The Ministry of The Assembly

CAROLINE M. THOMAS

RESOURCE PUBLICATIONS, INC.
San Jose, California

Nihil Obstat
23 February 2008
Imprimatur
23 February 2008

Reverend Monsignor Francis V. Cilia
Vicar General, Diocese of San Jose

© 2008 Resource Publications, Inc. All rights reserved. No part of this book may be photocopied or otherwise reproduced without permission from the publisher. For reprint permission, contact:

Reprint Department
Resource Publications, Inc.
160 E. Virginia St. #290
San Jose, CA 95112-5876
(408) 286-8505 ▪ (408) 287-8748 fax

Library of Congress Cataloging-in-Publication Data

Thomas, Caroline M., 1943-
 The ministry of the assembly / Caroline M. Thomas.
   p. cm.
 Includes bibliographical references.
 ISBN 978-0-89390-675-7 (pbk.)
 1. Public worship--Catholic Church. 2. Catholic Church--Liturgy. I. Title.
 BX1970.15.T56 2008
 264'.02--dc22
                                     2008020556

Printed in the United States of America
08 09 10 11 12 | 5 4 3 2 1

Cover illustration: George Collopy
Illustrations: George Collopy and Helen St Paul
Book design and production: Kenneth Guentert, The Publishing Pro, LLC
Copyeditor: Kenneth Guentert

Excerpts from the English translation of *The Roman Missal* © 1973, International Committee on English in the Liturgy, Inc. (ICEL); excerpts from the English translation of *The General Instruction of the Roman Missal* © 2002, ICEL. All rights reserved.

Contents

Preface	vi
Introduction	1
Chapter One: Looking at Liturgy	4
Chapter Two: Ministry	8
Chapter Three: We Gather	11
Chapter Four: We Listen	16
Chapter Five: We Respond	23
Chapter Six: We Are Sent Forth	41
Chapter Seven: The Assembly as an Initiating Community	44
Chapter Eight: What Are These Things?	46
Chapter Nine: Liturgical Seasons	50
Conclusion	56
Selected Bibliography	57

Preface

This book is about us, the inhabitants of the pews. It is a practical book, looking at our role as ministering members of the assembly. What is our part, and to a certain extent, what does it mean?

As this book is written, a revision of the sacramentary (also called the Roman Missal), the book of prayers used at Mass, is being undertaken by the bishops in union with Rome. Some changes in text are being considered. The responses mentioned in this book are the responses in use at this time. With a change in the sacramentary, some slight textual changes may result in our part, but the basic meanings will remain the same. Our roles during the various parts of the Mass will remain the same.

Introduction

Ever since Vatican Council II, we have heard that the changes in liturgy were intended to bring about the "conscious, active, and full participation" (*General Instruction of the Roman Missal* #18) of the assembly. But what does this mean? Mostly, the phrase has been interpreted to mean that the people are supposed to sing. As a result, much effort has gone into composing new music in the vernacular and introducing it into the liturgy. In addition, the assembly has been expected to recite aloud certain prayers of the liturgy. But this is just scratching the surface.

As a result of the Vatican Council, an entire mindset had to be changed. Before the Council, the Mass was in Latin, which for the most part was understood only by the priest. A dedicated few purchased missals written in English and Latin so they could follow the prayers. Most read devotional prayers or said the rosary. We described what was going on by saying that the priest "said Mass" while we "heard Mass" or "attended Mass." As we described the action of the Mass, the priest's role was active, the assembly's role was passive.

Since the Vatican Council, we have returned to our origins and now say that liturgy is the "work of the people." We now have speaking and singing parts. The most obvious changes were the repositioning of the altar facing the people, with the priest behind it, and the replacement of Latin with the vernacular so that we can readily understand and respond. Because the format of the Mass remains the same, these changes could be seen as superficial. Actually, the change is profound. It is a return to the spirit of the liturgy in the early church.

Imagine the very early church. Christians gathered once a week to follow Christ's command. They chose someone to lead them in prayer, to "preside." They weren't passive observers. They prayed together, led by the one they had chosen. They spoke a common language and had a common understanding that they were gathering to break the bread in Jesus' memory.

Over the centuries, the Mass became more formal. The language of liturgy, which probably was Aramaic or Hebrew at first, then Greek and Latin, remained Latin for centuries—hence the name "Latin Rite" for the largest segment of the Roman Catholic Church. This was the church's attempt to remain consistent. As Latin ceased being spoken colloquially, it stopped changing. It had no ambiguous idioms or phrases or words that changed meaning. Eventually, the people, for the most part, ceased to understand it.

In time, the church emphasized the sacrificial aspect of the Mass and the meal aspect diminished in the liturgical consciousness. The sacredness of the sacrifice assumed primary importance, and eventually only the priest was allowed to touch the consecrated bread and wine. The role of the assembly became more and more passive and restricted. The Mass, as originally instituted, was no longer the assembly's action but that of the ordained ministers and acolytes.

This is in part what Vatican Council II changed. The action of the celebration of Mass was given back to the people. There were other changes. The liturgy was divested of unnecessary repetitions and of superfluous actions and prayers, which had accumulated through the centuries. The Roman Rite, which more clearly showed the meaning of the liturgical celebration, was mostly restored to its "noble simplicity."

Today, the liturgy includes more Scripture texts. Whereas before the Council there were only two readings, now there are three. Instead of repeating the same readings every year, the liturgy now proceeds through a three-year cycle of readings for Sundays and a two-year cycle for weekdays. Celebrations of the sacraments have been restored to earlier forms that include Scripture readings.

The people are allowed to receive the consecrated host in their own hands, instead of being "fed" by the priest. Eventually, the reception of the sacred Blood was also restored to the people. All of these changes were part of the plan to return the liturgy (and Sacred Scripture) to the members of the assembly and to emphasize their—*our*—importance in the celebration.

In this book we will explore what this means in practical terms, what ministry means, how it can be said that being a member of the assembly is a ministry, and what relationship that ministry has to the others within the liturgy. We will look at the role and responsibilities of the assembly in the liturgy and beyond.

For the most part, this book assumes the "usual" weekend liturgy. Weekday Masses omit the Gloria and Creed and have only two readings unless the day is a special feast or solemnity. On special occasions—funerals, weddings, Masses with baptisms, and Palm Sunday, for example—other introductory rites transition directly to the Opening Prayer and take the place of the Act of Penance (formerly called the Penitential Rite) and the Gloria.

Chapter One
Looking at Liturgy

Importance of the Sunday Assembly

The assembly gathered together to praise God in Christ's name through the power of the Holy Spirit forms Christ's Body, the church. In the action of the eucharistic assembly—listening to God's word, responding in thanksgiving, and sharing the sacred Body and Blood—the church becomes what it is meant to be: a sacrament, a visible sign of Christ's presence in the world.

Christ in his physical form as a human being showed us who God is in human form. Christ is no longer present in his human form so it is the church which makes Christ *physically* present to the world. And while each of us is a member of the Body, it is only when we come together with each other that we become the united Body of Christ, the church.

When the members of Christ's Body gather together, we share our faith with one another and strengthen one another through our faith witness. In gathering as members of the assembly, we come as individuals, not for what we can "get out of it," but for what we can share with the other members. In this sharing, we are all strengthened and grow in faith and love.

The Real Presence of Christ

Historically, the church has always taught the real presence of Christ in the Eucharist, the consecrated bread and wine. Vatican II specified a broader notion of real presence. "Christ is really present in the very liturgical assembly gathered in his name, in the person of the minister, in his word, and indeed substantially and continuously under the eucharistic species." (GIRM #27) In other words, one of the primary forms in which Christ is truly present is in the gathered assembly, his Body.

Putting the Mass Together

The liturgy has two main parts, the Liturgy of the Word, and the Liturgy of the Eucharist. In the first we listen to God's Word, in the second we respond to it in praise and thanksgiving. Before the Liturgy of the Word is the Introductory Rite, during which we gather, and following the Liturgy of the Eucharist is the Concluding Rite, which sends us forth to serve. In total, there are four sections to the liturgy, two main parts and two "framing" parts, one introductory and one concluding. In essence, we gather, we listen, we respond, and we are sent forth.

Ritual Is Not Boring

Two characteristics of liturgy help to enable our participation. The first is that liturgy is a ritual action. This helps us, as members of the assembly, to know our part. The action does not vary much from week to week, and we can do our part with confidence. If things changed constantly in each liturgy, we wouldn't know what was expected of us, and it would be hard to participate. Ritual makes liturgy safe and comfortable. The danger is that our participation might become thoughtless.

Liturgy Is a Dialogue

The second aspect of liturgy is that it is a dialogue. This means that liturgy has a call-and-response format. One example of this, which is also an example of ritual action, is the following dialogue. The presider says, "The Lord be with you." And the assembly says, "And also with you." The response is known and automatic, a ritual. It is a call and response.

The dialogue characteristic of the liturgy is found not only in the brief exchanges between presider and assembly but also within the parts of the liturgy itself. Within the Liturgy of the Word, we listen to the Word and respond with the singing of the psalm. We respond to the readings and homily with the Creed and the Prayers of the Faithful. Our response to the Liturgy of the Word, to the story of what God has done for us in the past, is a response of praise and thanksgiving: the Liturgy of the Eucharist. In other words, the second major part of the liturgy is a response to the first major part. As I examine the individual parts of the Mass, I will discuss this in more detail. As you can see, our part in the liturgy has grown since the Council. There is more for us to be conscious of and to do.

Postures and Actions

There are three major postures during the liturgy. Each speaks of its own interior attitude and has its own appropriate use.

Standing is the traditional posture of Jewish prayer and praise. It is a posture of attentiveness, respect, and readiness to serve. Eucharistic Prayer II says, "We thank you for counting us worthy to stand in your presence and serve you."

Sitting is the posture of receptivity and sometimes of rest. We are seated to listen to the words of Scripture (except the Gospel) and to listen to the homily. We open ourselves to hear and receive the Word in which Christ is truly present.

Kneeling is a posture of adoration, submission, penance, and repentance. It is also a very personal posture. When we kneel, we draw more into ourselves and tend to be less connected with those around us.

Besides the postures, there are many actions that we perform during the liturgy. For example, we sign ourselves with the sign of the cross. We greet each other with the sign of peace. We bow during the Creed, during the Institution Narrative (if we are standing), and when we approach to receive communion. We participate in several processions. We process into the church building at the beginning. We process up during communion. We process out into the world at the dismissal. In addition, some members of the assembly may participate in the gospel procession and in a procession to bring up the gifts. In many parishes, all the members of the community process to bring up their gifts.

Chapter Two
Ministry

What Is Ministry?

In brief, ministry is service. Jesus was the prime example of service. At the Last Supper, when he washed his apostles' feet, his command was that we serve one another as he had served. The priest is often described as a "minister," although to a large extent this is meant to suggest that he is the one who officiates at the liturgy, not one who serves. The lectors, extraordinary ministers of Holy Communion, ushers, greeters, and musicians, are also called "ministers." Again, this is usually meant to suggest some public role played within the liturgy. For all of these, it is important to remember that the basic definition of ministry is service. All these ministerial roles exist to serve all the members of the Body. Even the role of the priest, whom we call the "presider," is defined in the context of the assembly.

All ministers, including the presider, are first and foremost members of the assembly. When they are not functioning in their specific ministerial roles, all minister to one another as members of the assembly. From the assembly, some are called forth to serve in a specific role according to their gifts and talents. Ideally, they are called forth by the members of the community to serve that specific community. And those who do not serve as lectors, musicians, and so on, are they ministers? Absolutely!

We are all called to minister to one another, through our witness of faith, through our participation, and through our response and responsiveness to those who are the "public" ministers. We all have responsibility to minister to one another within the liturgy and beyond. The source of our responsibility? Baptism. We were all baptized into Christ as priest, prophet, and king. Within the Jewish tradition, priest, prophet, and king are all roles of service to God's people.

Through our actions as participating members of the assembly, we support and encourage one another. We strengthen one another's faith. We strengthen the Body, the church. We enable the gifts of the other ministries. We serve the world through our priestly ministry of intercessory prayer.

There are Many Gifts ...

Those who have been called to specific public ministerial roles within the liturgy need to be trained for their part in the celebration. In the case of the music ministers particularly, there are usually many years of preparation needed to achieve the proficiency required to lead God's people in song. Lectors, even if naturally gifted in public speaking, still must study and pray the Scriptures before they can proclaim God's Word, witness to their own faith, and call forth the faith of their listeners. Extraordinary ministers of Holy Communion need to go through their own training, both in understanding of their ministry and in the procedures of the individual parish. For example, they may be expected to arrive early for set up and to stay after Mass to put the vessels away and so forth. Greeters and ushers also need formation in their roles and at the very least need to arrive early to be sure all is ready for the members of the assembly. They need to remain after Mass to restore the church building to its previous state of neatness, cleanliness, and readiness for God's people. Altar servers need to go through training in ministry and in procedure. The presider, of course, must spend many years of study and prayer in preparation for his role. Even those who work behind the scenes—those who set up the environment or clean the linens or dust the fixtures—must be trained to do these things in order to help God's people focus on their prayer.

Preparation for the Ministry of the Assembly

We've seen that all the leadership ministries require advance training and proximate preparation. What about preparation for the ministry of the assembly? Is any needed?

There are three ways we can prepare:

By becoming informed about the liturgy so that we can participate more easily in the opportunities presented in each part of the Mass. Reading this book is a form of such preparation.

By familiarizing ourselves with the lectionary readings before coming to Mass. By reflecting on these readings, we make them our own and thus bring something of our own contemplation to the hearing of the Word and the homily.

By giving ourselves suitable time to prepare for Mass so that we don't arrive harried and hassled. This includes dressing appropriately and respectfully for the occasion. (Remember where the expression "Sunday best" came from.) In so doing, we come prepared to do the intense work of liturgy.

The next four chapters will focus on:

Doing the Work of Liturgy

Chapter Three
We Gather

This chapter begins an examination of each part of the Mass with reference to the role of the members of the assembly. This particular chapter focuses on the Introductory Rites. The function of the Introductory Rites is to gather us together as a worshiping community and to prepare us to listen and respond. As we celebrate the Introductory Rites, we are changed from a group of individuals into a unified body, the assembly, coming together in response to God's call.

Gathering

The gathering begins before we even reach the church building. It begins at home as we get ready and continues as we make our way to church. Ideally, on the way from the parking lot, we will greet people and begin to form into an assembly, the worshiping body. In the Western world, people tend to view themselves as individuals who happen to be coming together for a common purpose. However, from a theological perspective, we *are* a community, a people called together as one, the Body of Christ, acting in union with one another for the common good of all and for the world.

Blessing Ourselves with Holy Water

One of the first things we do upon entering the church building is to bless ourselves with water from the holy water font. In many parishes, members of the assembly come into the building past the actual baptismal font.

Blessing ourselves with water from the font reminds us of our baptism, that we became members of this community, part of God's family, through the waters of baptism. Because this gesture can become an automatic action, it is important to take a moment to reflect on the meaning of the water and of the gesture. We were baptized in the name of the Father, the Son, and the Holy Spirit. This is what we commemorate and affirm each time we bless ourselves.

Entrance Procession

When we enter the church building, we are part of the entrance procession. People often think of the entrance procession as the ministers coming in just before the start of Mass, but the procession *begins* when the first members of the assembly enter the building and *culminates* with the formal procession of ministers. Some parishes are built with a large indoor gathering space, which enables everyone to mingle and greet one another and then process in together. Most parishes do this at the Easter Vigil, when we all process in after the lighting of the Easter fire. They also do it on Palm Sunday, when the palms are distributed and blessed outside, and all process in following those Introductory Rites.

During the entrance procession, the Book of Gospels is processed up. Part of the reason we stand at this time is to joyfully greet the Word of God come among us. Our standing is an expression of our excitement. At the end of the liturgy, the Book of Gospels is not processed out. We, the people of God, take the living Word with us as we go.

On some occasions, especially special feast days, we use incense at various times during the liturgy to express reverence. One of the times it may be used is during the entrance procession. The incense is prayerfully carried through the assembly—because the assembly is a sign of Christ's presence—and brought to the front where the altar is incensed.

Entrance Song

During the formal entrance procession, we sing the entrance song. This is more than music to accompany the movement of the ministers up the aisle. The song sets the focus for the day, echoing the readings or the feast or season. Within the Introductory Rites, the entrance song is especially suited to gather us. Some parishes even refer to it as the "gathering song."

By any name, the entrance song has a unifying effect, causing all of us to act together as one worshiping community, so much so that we even breathe in unison. Because the song is not just "walking music," it should not end when the presider has reached his station in front of the assembly. Presumably, he has participated in the singing during the procession and continues to sing with us after reaching the sanctuary. This helps create the experience that we are all joining together—presider, ministers, assembly. This forming of community is the work of all, and all should participate. For the same reason, the entrance song should not be left up to the musicians. As members of the assembly, *we* are the primary ministers of music. The job of those who serve in front as musicians is to lead us in our ministry of music.

Sign of the Cross

The presider's first words are to lead us in the sign of the cross. This reminds us that we do this as we do everything: in the name of the Trinity, the Father, Son, and Holy Spirit. The prayers of the liturgy are offered to the Father, in the name of the Son, by the power of the Holy Spirit. We sign ourselves and consciously dedicate ourselves anew. Our response is "Amen." This is the first of many responses.

Greeting

The presider addresses us with, "The Lord be with you," or one of the longer greetings. This greeting verbalizes the truth of the Lord's presence in the gathered assembly. We continue the dialogue, as we return our greeting, "And also with you." We may even use a gesture of extending our hands toward the presider as we respond. At this time the presider may say a few words about the feast being celebrated to introduce us to the specifics of the day's celebration.

Act of Penitence

This used to be called the penitential rite. It reminds us that although we are sinners, God has saved us. We may recite the Confiteor or the Kyrie, which is a litany of praise for God's mercy. As we join in these prayers, we verbally acknowledge our sinfulness and God's mercy.

The Rite of Blessing and Sprinkling of Water

Instead of the Act of Penitence, this rite can be used. As the presider sprinkles us with holy water, we are reminded of our salvation through the waters of baptism. In acknowledgment and affirmation of this, we sign ourselves with the sign of the cross as we gladly feel the drops of water.

The Gloria

This is a hymn of praise, which is part of the liturgy on Sundays and special feasts. Although the sacramentary states that it is to be "said or sung," there is a strong preference for this hymn to be sung. The Gloria is an opportunity for us to join in the Christmas angels' song of praise with full voice and heart.

In the case of a funeral Mass, Mass with a baptism, or any other Mass where there is a specific introductory ritual, the Act of Penitence and Gloria are omitted. During Lent, a solemn penitential season, the Gloria is omitted. It is also omitted during Advent as we withhold the joyous song so that it may resound more fully as we celebrate the incarnation at Christmas.

The Opening Prayer or Collect

The name "Opening Prayer" can be misleading because it is not the first prayer of the liturgy. Rather, it is the first of the presidential prayers, that is, prayers voiced by the presider. Also, what the presider says is not the whole prayer. First he says, "Let us pray." Because the presider often begins his part of the Opening Prayer as soon as the server brings him the book, the pause after the invitation to pray may seem designed simply to allow the server time to come over with the book. Actually, the pause is part of the invitation to pray. In the early church, that's what members of the assembly did, usually aloud. After the assembly voiced its prayer, the presider said the conclusion to its prayer. His conclusion came to be called the "Collect" because he collected all of the assembly's prayers and brought them to summation.

The presider's invitation to pray is still directed to us. When we hear "Let us pray," it is an invitation for us to pray. We no longer say it aloud, but we form our intentions silently. Then when the presider says the Opening Prayer, it includes all that we have intended in our hearts. So, instead of simply watching the altar server bring the book, we should form our intentions and open our hearts to God. Then, after the Collect, we give a heartfelt "Amen" to voice our involvement and assent.

This concludes the Introductory Rites. Their purpose has been to form us into a worshiping community that acts as a united body and to prepare us for the main parts of the liturgy to come.

Chapter Four
We Listen

After the Introductory Rites, we are all seated in a posture of receptivity to listen to the story of God's action in our human history. We call this The Liturgy of the Word. It begins with the first reading and extends through the general intercessions. Since Vatican II, this has been referred to as the "table of the Word." This term, which is parallel to the "eucharistic table," expresses the capacity of the Word to nourish us.

The First Reading

This reading is usually from the Old Testament. During the Easter season, the first reading is taken from the Acts of the Apostles. Although there are historical elements to many of these readings, the writers primarily were testifying to how they understood God to be working in history and in their lives.

The lector "proclaims" the reading. This suggests something more than "reading." Proclamation is a faith witness. The Word becomes alive in our midst as it is proclaimed by a living person. Presumably, the lector has spent the last week with the reading in prayer, practice, and even study, so that he or she can communicate the message specifically to this community on this day. Our job is to listen actively. This means more than paying attention. It means looking at the lector and being an attentive, receptive gathering of listeners. We know from our own experience what it is like if people are not looking at us when we speak to them. The same is true for the lectors. Ideally, they are looking at us as they proclaim the Word. If we have our eyes in a missalette, full communication between speaker and listener cannot happen. It is our job to encourage and support the reader with attentive eye contact. Lectoring does not happen in a vacuum. The lector is speaking to us, and it is important that it is obvious we are listening. This is part of our ministry to them.

Silence

Following the reading, there should be a brief period of silence. This is a time for us to absorb the Word we have heard and to reflect on it to make it our own. Normally, this period of silence occurs again after the second reading as well as after the homily.

Responsorial Psalm

This is our opportunity to respond to God's word. However, the name "responsorial" does not refer to this fact but to the responsorial format of the psalm. The cantor sings the antiphon; we respond by repeating it, at the beginning and after each verse. The cantor invites our song. We must do our part. Ideally, the cantor does not sing our part or sings only softly away from the microphone. That way, we can more easily hear ourselves responding together, and it is more obvious that the response is our part.

The Responsorial Psalm focuses us. It has been described as the aura in which we understand the whole Liturgy of the Word for the day. Indeed, the antiphon, as written in the lectionary, reflects the focus of the readings and helps to clarify it for us. It is permissible, for pastoral reasons, to use a seasonal psalm, instead of the psalm for the day. This makes our participation a little easier. However, because the same psalm response is repeated from week to week, it does not give the same fine focus to help us better understand the readings of the week.

The Second Reading

This reading is always taken from the New Testament, usually from one of the letters of St. Paul or one of the other apostles. Again, this is the faith witness of the early church as its members experienced Christ's presence and God's work in their midst. Once again, the lector, after careful preparation, proclaims this reading to our specific community at this particular time. Once again, our work is attentive listening, encouraging and supporting the lector in his or her ministry through our eye contact and posture. We listen eagerly to what God has given us to hear on this day. This listening part of the liturgy should take energy because we are in fact ministering to the lector through our active participation in the Liturgy of the Word.

The Alleluia or Gospel Acclamation

This joyful acclamation is not a response to what has gone before but an eager anticipation of hearing the Gospel. It is processional music, although on most Sundays the procession is minimal, usually consisting of carrying the book from the altar to the ambo. In some parishes and on some feast days, there is an extended procession, sometimes accompanied by candles and incense. We leap to our feet in joyous acclamation of the Word of God, Christ Jesus, present in the Gospel. In these various ways we show our reverence for the Gospel and honor Christ present in his Word. Yes! We are ready to listen!

The format of the Gospel Acclamation is usually: an Alleluia sung by the cantor and repeated by the assembly; a brief verse, hinting at the content of the full reading, sung by cantor or choir; the Alleluia repeated again by the assembly. During Lent, the word, Alleluia, is not used. This word is "retired" for Lent, and the somberness of the season is emphasized by an acclamation such as, "Praise to you, Lord Jesus Christ, King of endless glory." This allows the Alleluia to be sung all the more joyously at Easter.

However, even in this more somber season, we stand and sing an acclamation to honor the Gospel and express our readiness to hear it.

The Gospel

The reading of the Gospel is the high point of the Liturgy of the Word. It begins with a dialogue between the Gospel reader and the assembly.

"The Lord be with you."

"And also with you."

"A reading from the holy gospel according to Matthew [or Mark, Luke or John]."

"Glory to you, Lord."

The sacramentary directs the proclaimer of the Gospel to make the sign of the cross on his forehead, lips, and over his heart. This has gradually become the ritual of the members of the assembly as well, and the most recent GIRM now indicates that "everyone else" does this gesture. They pray that the words of the Gospel be in their minds, on their lips, and in their hearts.

If incense is used, the book is incensed at this time, honoring the words as those of Christ himself.

As we did with the lector during the first two readings, we support the proclaimer of the Gospel with our eye contact and conscious, active attention. When the proclaimer looks out at us, he should know that he has our full involvement. Our attentiveness should encourage him in his faith-filled proclamation. We stand at attention, like servants awaiting our master's commands.

At the conclusion to the reading, the proclaimer says, "The gospel of the Lord." We enthusiastically respond, "Praise to you, Lord Jesus Christ."

Sometimes, the words of the Gospel seem to be hard, or confusing, and we aren't inclined to have such a joyful response. Still, it is Christ's presence that we honor. The homily will, ideally, clarify and illuminate for us how this word can benefit us in our daily living.

The proclaimer then kisses the book from which he has proclaimed the Gospel. In many parishes the book is now positioned in a place of honor.

The Homily

People used to refer to this as the sermon. At that time, it could be a talk about any religious topic on which the preacher wished to speak. With Vatican II the homily was reinstated as an application of the reading to the lives of the people. The *General Instruction of the Roman Missal* allows that the homily may also be focused on another text of the day's liturgy.

Again, our ministry is to support and encourage the homilist through our attentive listening. In this way, the homily is interactive. Many homilists report that the responsiveness of the assembly energizes their homily. Just as in a conversation it is difficult to speak to someone who is not paying attention, the same is true for the homilist. Attentive faces, smiles or laughs when appropriate, a nod of agreement, all help the homilist in his ministry. In some Christian traditions, it is customary to encourage the homilist with an occasional "Amen" from the members of the assembly. Most Catholic parishes don't respond out loud, but we can still signal our assent, approval, or understanding non-verbally.

After the homily, the homilist usually is seated for a few moments to allow time for reflection. This is our time to assimilate what we have heard and perhaps to make an intention to apply it in our lives, possibly even to make changes.

The Profession of Faith (Creed)

Now it's our time to respond and give our assent to what we have heard during the Liturgy of the Word. We stand to physically affirm our beliefs in the Nicene Creed, the Apostles' Creed, or on occasion, the Renewal of Baptismal Promises. We recall the teachings of the church before beginning the Liturgy of the Eucharist. We bow at the words, "by the power of the Holy Spirit he was born of the Virgin Mary, and became man" to physically demonstrate our awe and appreciation for this central tenet of our Christian faith.

The Prayer of the Faithful

In the early church, this was called the "Prayer of the Faithful" because only those who had been baptized could stay for this part of the liturgy. In fact, the catechumens were dismissed before the recitation of the Creed. The Profession of Faith was connected to baptism, and reciting this affirmation of faith with the community was reserved for those who had been baptized. Thus, the liturgy up to the Creed was at that time called "The Mass of the Catechumens." The second half, from the Creed on, was called "The Mass of the Faithful." Before the catechumenate was restored by Vatican II, this distinction was lost because there were no catechumens to dismiss, and everyone stayed for the entire liturgy. This litany of intercessions came to be called the "General Intercessions." With the restoration of the Order of Catechumens, those preparing for baptism are once again dismissed before the Creed and go to reflect more deeply on the Word of God that they have heard. Only at their baptism do they begin to recite the Creed with us, participate in the intercessions, and remain for the rest of the liturgy.

The general intercessions belong to the faithful, to those already baptized, because it was through baptism into the priesthood of Christ that the faithful are granted the right and responsibility to pray for the intentions of the world. We exercise our baptismal priesthood in these prayers. They are called "general" intercessions because they are to be for the needs of the world. We've heard God's word proclaimed in the readings and homily, we see the ideal that God wants for the world, and we see the discrepancy in what truly exists. Therefore, we exercise our priestly ministry in praying for the fulfillment of God's will for the situations in the world. We pray first for the needs of the universal church, then for those of the world. We pray for those who are in need in any way. We pray for the needs of our local parish and community. This usually includes those who are sick and those who have died. We include any special celebrations or events. This is the structure the church has given us.

In the format of this litany, the presider first invites us to prayer with an introduction. Then the deacon, cantor, lector, or another person introduces the intentions. There should be a pause after each intention before the words, "we pray to the Lord," or whatever formula is used. This gives us time to make the intention our own and to silently add to it anything that we wish to include. Then, after the leader invites our response, we say or sing, "Lord, hear our prayer" or another similar phrase. This is actually the prayer. Our response. Not the invitation to prayer. Not the statement of the intentions but our making the intention our own and asking the Lord to hear our prayer. That's the prayer part. Then, the presider says the concluding prayer, which sums it all up. We respond "Amen" to seal it with our assent.

Chapter Five
We Respond

The entire celebration takes its name from this next part—The Liturgy of the Eucharist! Eucharist means thanksgiving. Our response to God's action in our lives and history, which we have heard in the readings and homily, is to give God thanks and praise.

The Preparation of the Gifts

This is a low-key time of the Mass. We are seated and rest from the work we have done, but we are still preparing for the work ahead. We used to call this time the offertory, but since Vatican II, it has been called the "preparation of gifts." This is partly in recognition of the fact that the actual offering of the liturgy takes place after the consecration. We'll get to that later.

During the preparation of the gifts, we may sing a song focusing on the readings or feast of the day, or the choir may sing, or there may be an instrumental piece. However, music is not essential to the ritual at this point. The collection is taken up, which is our physical participation in the preparation of the gifts. We give the common medium of today's commerce, a fiscal donation. In many parishes, the members of the assembly process up themselves to place their donation in baskets. Sometimes there are baskets to receive items for the needy as well. This is more reminiscent of what it was like in the early church. While the collection is being taken up, or processed up, the altar is being prepared.

This is usually done by the altar servers. If a deacon is present, he prepares the altar, assisted by the servers. They place the corporal and sacramentary (the book with the priest's prayers) on the altar, along with a chalice and purificator.

Our part has been our financial contribution, including a procession up with our gifts if that is the custom in our parish, and participating in the singing if a communal song is used, or prayerful listening if a choir anthem or instrumental piece is used.

The Presentation of the Gifts

To culminate the preparation of the gifts, someone who has been designated processes up with the bread and wine for the sacrificial meal. These are the only gifts that will be placed on the altar because they are the ones to be used in the rite. The money is also processed up at this time and usually placed in front of the altar. If it has been collected in front by a procession of the assembly, it is consolidated and placed out of the way of the communion procession, perhaps in front of the altar.

The song, if there is one, continues throughout, even during the silent prayers. Once the gifts are placed on the altar we are ready to begin the eucharistic celebration. We unite ourselves with the gifts, presenting ourselves, also, for transformation.

The presider says prayers over the gifts. They are patterned after Jewish table prayers of thanksgiving. The focus is on thanksgiving for the gifts, which, as the prayers say, are fruit of the earth and work of our hands. In other words, they are something given by God and formed by our human hands. This prayer is meant to be said silently. If there is no music at this time, the prayers may be said audibly, in which case we respond with a wholehearted, "Blessed be God for ever."

The Mixing of Wine and Water

As part of preparing the wine a few drops of water are added to it. This was a custom that derived from the heavy texture of the wine in ancient times. Water was always added to dilute it. Christians continued to do this, and eventually it came to be interpreted as symbolic of the union of Christ's human and divine natures, of Christ's union with the church, or of our share in the divine sonship of Christ.

This particular action used to be given more importance in the liturgy, but since Vatican II it has been accompanied by the presider's brief silent prayer: "By the mystery of this water and wine may we come to share in the divinity of Christ, who humbled himself to share in our humanity."

Incensing the Gifts

On special occasions, the gifts and the altar are incensed at this time. The cross, if near the altar, is also incensed. If there is a deacon or other minister, he will incense the priest. Then we also stand and are incensed. All that are incensed are signs of Christ and Christ's presence. All are honored.

Washing of the Hands

If incense has been used, there is a practical reason for the priest to wash his hands at this point. At most Masses, where incense is not used, the washing of the hands remains as a reminder of the days when the presentation of the gifts included eggs, chickens, cabbages, or whatever was given to share with the community. It has also been traditionally understood as an outward expression of a prayer for interior purification.

Invitation and Prayer Over the Gifts

At this time the presider invites us all to join him in the prayer that is to follow. Our response: "May the Lord accept the sacrifice at your hands for the praise and glory of his name, for our good, and the good of all his Church," symbolizes our involvement in the prayer and our connection to the priest who voices it. With this response we verify that we wish the presider to continue the liturgical prayer in our name. At this time we stand, ready to begin the intense work of the Liturgy of the Eucharist. The presider continues with the brief prayer over the gifts to which we respond, "Amen."

THE EUCHARISTIC PRAYER
Dialogue

The Eucharistic Prayer begins with a dialogue between priest and people. Ideally this dialogue is sung, in which case we sing our response with full voice.

"The Lord be with you."

"And also with you."

"Lift up your hearts."

"We lift them up to the Lord."

"Let us give thanks to the Lord our God."

"It is right to give him thanks and praise."

This exchange begins the great prayer of thanksgiving. We encourage the presider with our strong response, whether sung or spoken. In some parishes, the people gesture towards the presider when they say, "And also with you." They might also lift their hands when they respond, "We lift them up to the Lord." Although these gestures are not prescribed for the people, they can facilitate entering the prayer more fully.

Preface

The priest now says or sings the Preface. This is not like the preface of a book, even though it does precede the rest of the Eucharistic Prayer. Here, the word "preface" is used because it is said "before the face" of God.

With this prayer, we are beginning to sing God's praise. We must listen carefully, especially for three things, or this prayer will flow right over us. First, this prayer changes according to the season or feast, and it can be different each week. Second, the Preface praises God for what God has done for us. It sets the scene, reminds God of God's history of goodness, so that, based on our past experience, we can petition God to continue showing goodness to us. Third, the presider, as in all of his prayers, speaks in first person plural. It's not "I" but "we."

The priest is the one voicing the prayers aloud, but they are our prayers, too. And mentally, we need to be right with him, saying these prayers in our hearts. This whole celebration is the work of the people, and so we need to be doing our part. Because the priest has been called to lead us in our prayer, he is the one whose voice we hear. The Preface is, however, no less our prayer. That use of the second-person plural is a constant reminder of the fact that these prayers belong to all of us.

Holy, Holy, Holy

Now we get to sing (or only in very rare circumstances, recite) the Holy, Holy, Holy. Because our response to the Preface is normally the sung Holy, Holy, Holy, the dialogue nature of the exchange between presider and assembly is more obvious if the Preface is sung as well.

The text of the prayer is taken from the book of Isaiah the prophet and the Palm Sunday entrance into Jerusalem in the Gospel of Matthew. This is a song of great joy and praise. It is the first of the "eucharistic acclamations." If nothing else is sung during the liturgy, the eucharistic acclamations should be sung. They are the actual text of the ritual itself. The music is not an add-on. It is integral to the rite. We sing out strongly to demonstrate our joy in the God who saves us. We praise God with zeal and energy in our gratitude.

To Stand or Not to Stand …

The *General Instruction of the Roman Missal* (#43) states that the assembly stands from the invitation before the prayer over the gifts until the end of Mass with some exceptions. However, for the dioceses of the United States of America an indult (exception) has been granted, which directs that the assembly kneel following the Holy, Holy, Holy until after the Great Amen. A further exception is made for reasons of lack of space, personal health, or "some other good reason." This allows for a different posture, such as standing or, in the case of ill health or other concerns, sitting.

During the Eucharistic Prayer, *the* prayer of praise and thanksgiving, it is more difficult to maintain the feeling of unity and communal participation in the kneeling posture because kneeling tends to put us into a more introspective mode. If kneeling is the posture in the parish, we must concentrate more intentionally on maintaining an attitude of community prayer and continuing to be active in our prayerful participation.

Further into the Eucharistic Prayer

Some of the Eucharistic Prayers are shorter than others. Unfortunately, due to time constraints, the shorter ones are frequently used. Eucharistic Prayer IV is one of the most beautiful. It tells salvation history in abbreviated form, and sets the scene for the heart of this great prayer. If the shorter forms are used, we need to focus more deliberately or this very meaningful and densely packed prayer will slip past us before we truly enter into it. The presider can help. If he says this prayer slowly and includes brief pauses between sentences, it is easier for us to hear the words and make them our own.

Epiclesis

This strange word meaning "invocation" names the prayer which invokes the power of the Holy Spirit to come upon the gifts of bread and wine to transform them into Christ's Body and Blood. This is an important point. The priest, with the authority given him by ordination, speaks in the name of the church, in *our* name, to invoke the Holy Spirit on behalf of all of us. It is the power of the Holy Spirit that will transform the bread and wine into the Body and Blood of Christ. With the priest, we call on the Holy Spirit to act on our behalf.

Institution Narrative

This is the part of the liturgy that describes Jesus' actions and words at the Last Supper. After the words are spoken over the bread, the priest elevates the large host slightly to show it to the community, and then genuflects. Those who are standing make a "profound" bow to coincide with the priest's genuflection. The same pattern is followed with the words over the wine. Our bow indicates our reverence for Christ's presence in the consecrated bread and wine.

Memorial Acclamation

Following the second genuflection during the institution narrative, the presider invites us to vocally affirm our acceptance of the paschal mystery. This expresses our belief in the mystery of Christ's life, death, resurrection and presence among us. It is called the Memorial Acclamation. This is the second of the eucharistic acclamations. Most frequently used is this wording: "Christ has died, Christ is risen, Christ will come again." There are three other formulas used to proclaim this mystery. Most often they are sung. This is an important way for us to witness to our faith. Again, the sung response is integral to the liturgy. It is our "out loud" part in the dialogue of the Eucharistic Prayer. A sung invitation by the presider encourages our sung response.

The Anamnesis

Another strange word for our new vocabulary, *anamnesis,* means "remembrance." This Greek word has a deeper meaning in the liturgical context than the English translation suggests. It refers not only to events in the past, which we remember, but also to the continuing effect of these events in our *present* lives. This paschal mystery of Jesus Christ, which we celebrate and remember, is actively effective in our lives at this time. At the same time we acknowledge and look forward to the promise of future glory.

Offering

This is the part of the liturgy that is the actual offering. The gift offered is no less than Jesus Christ himself. In the words of Eucharistic Prayer IV, "…we offer you his body and blood, the acceptable sacrifice which brings salvation to the whole world." It is our gifts of bread and wine that have been transformed into this sacred Body and Blood, and we ourselves are symbolically offered with and through Jesus Christ. This should be our conscious intention.

At this time, the Holy Spirit is invoked one more time, this time upon us, Christ's Body. Eucharistic Prayer III asks that we may "become one body, one spirit in Christ." Eucharistic Prayer IV asks the Holy Spirit to "gather all who share this one bread and one cup into the one body of Christ, a living sacrifice of praise." As we listen to the presider's words, we join with him in a desire to become more closely united to Jesus Christ, the spotless victim who is the head of his Body, the church. We join with Christ in offering his sacrifice to the Father.

Intercessions

At this time the Eucharistic Prayer has intercessions for the pope, for the bishop, for all those participating in this prayer, for those who have died, for all the church and for the salvation of the world. This is an all-inclusive, universal prayer. Our hearts reach out with the words of the presider to all those for whom this sacrifice is offered. The words vary, depending on which Eucharistic Prayer is chosen. Our job is to join with conscious intention in this universal prayer of the church.

Doxology

The Eucharistic Prayer concludes with the Doxology, the hymn of praise, "Through him, with him, in him, in the unity of the Holy Spirit, all glory and honor is yours, almighty Father, for ever and ever."

Ideally, the Doxology is sung by the priest, although it is frequently recited. It sums up and concludes the Eucharistic Prayer with a trinitarian formula, acknowledging the active roles of Father, Son, and Holy Spirit. It leads into our most important response of the entire liturgy.

The Great Amen

Having heard the story of salvation history, the commemoration of Christ's saving life, death and resurrection on our behalf, and all the prayer that has gone before, we now give our final affirmation of all that has preceded in our sung "Amen!" We say, "Yes, we agree! This is what we believe!" This, the third of the eucharistic acclamations, is our most important response of the liturgy and should ring from the rafters. As the priest elevates the consecrated bread and wine, our voices should make it clear that this is a heartfelt, enthusiastic acclamation. As with the other acclamations, this one should be sung. If the priest sings the Doxology, the flow of the dialogue is more natural as the people respond in song.

THE COMMUNION RITE

This is the culmination of the Liturgy of the Eucharist. It begins with the Lord's Prayer and concludes with the prayer after communion. This is the part of the liturgy for which we have been preparing by all that has gone before.

The Lord's Prayer

Now we are invited to join together in the prayer that Jesus Christ gave to us through his apostles when they asked him how they were to pray. The Lord's Prayer can be recited or sung. If we think about the words as we say them, they prick our consciences. It is easy enough to pray for "our daily bread" but not so easy to pray with conviction that we be forgiven as we forgive others. To maintain integrity as we say these words, we must at this time resolve to forgive those against whom we have enmity, to let go of grudges, to open our hearts to all God's people.

Many parishes have the custom of holding hands during the Our Father. This seems to have developed as a physical expression of praying together to "our Father." It is a grass roots development, not one called for by the instructions in the Roman Missal.

The sacramentary calls for the priest to pray the Lord's Prayer with "hands extended." Many parishes invite the people to imitate the gesture of the presider and to extend their hands in the traditional prayer posture. We follow whichever is the custom in our parish.

Sign of Peace

Originally, this was called the "kiss of peace." It has occupied various locations during the liturgy and appears now just before communion. This is not an ordinary greeting but the wishing of Christ's peace upon one another. The presider (or deacon, if one is present) invites the people to exchange the sign of peace.

In most parishes, the priest used to exchange the sign of peace with the servers and anyone else in the sanctuary and then go to the community to exchange the sign of peace with those in the first row or two. In recent years, the instruction to the presider has changed. He is to remain in the sanctuary unless there is some special occasion, such as a wedding or funeral, where for pastoral reasons he would want to greet the family or other members of the assembly.

The reasoning for this change is that the peace of Christ does not belong only or mainly to the priest. It is for all of us to share with one another. If the priest appears to bring the peace down from the sanctuary, people might think that this peace is something he has and passes on to the rest of us. By not having the presider "bring the peace" to the members of the assembly, the new instruction emphasizes our role as the true presence of Christ. It is our task to bring the peace of Christ to one another. If for pastoral reasons, the presider comes to members of the assembly to exchange this sign, it is still our right and duty to exchange it with one another as baptized members of the Body of Christ. Depending on the culture and tradition in the parish as well as our familiarity with the people around us, the sign of peace can be a kiss, a hug, a handshake, a bow, or any other gesture that is meaningful to the participants.

This exchange of the sign of peace should be brief. We exchange the sign of peace only with those immediately around us. If we were to prolong this ritual by greeting people all around the church building, it would overshadow communion, which should be our primary experience of community. The sign of peace is preparatory to communion, an opportunity to emphasize our forgiving attitude and harmony before receiving the sacrament. It calls us to reconciliation and unity and prepares us for our ultimate communion with one another in the sacrament.

Breaking of the Bread/Lamb of God

In the early church, the eucharistic celebration was called the "Breaking of the Bread." This shows the emphasis that was placed on this part of the rite. The gesture of breaking the bread is important to the understanding of Eucharist. First, the bread is broken and the wine poured out in service, as we are also to be used in service to others. Second, the fact that we all receive from the one bread and cup, all sharing in the one bread of life, is essential in our understanding of our sacramental unity.

As things have developed through the centuries, there is usually only one large host, which the presider breaks. Most often the rest are small individual hosts which have been purchased, usually from a monastery or religious goods store. Unfortunately, neither the presider's host, nor the individual hosts usually look like the bread we use on our tables.

Christ's Last Supper was a celebration of Passover, the Feast of Unleavened Bread. This festival recalls how God brought the chosen people out of Egypt. He instructed them to bake their bread in a hurry so that they would be ready to leave. When we use unleavened bread, we remember Christ's Passover celebration and connect with God's saving action on behalf of the Israelites.

Church documents ask us to use bread that appears to be real food. In response to this directive, many parishes have started a bread-baking ministry. Using a recipe approved by the diocese, members of the community make the unleavened bread for the liturgy. The product that results is usually thicker and chewier in texture and has a true wheat bread flavor. These breads can be scored so that they break quickly during the liturgy. If necessary, some can be broken before Mass starts. Although there are some logistics to work out if real bread is used, the practice makes receiving Eucharist more like the actual meal it was intended to be.

Since Vatican II, the reception of the sacred Blood has been restored to the laity. The wine to be consecrated is brought up to the altar in a single container. This is now the sign of the "one cup," from which we all receive. Until recently, the wine was poured into the individual chalices for reception by the assembly at the same time the bread was broken, during the Lamb of God. Recent directives call for the wine to be poured before the consecration, at the preparation of the gifts time, to eliminate the danger of spilling the consecrated wine while pouring.

Nevertheless, the sign of receiving from one cup remains as we all process up to drink from a common cup. This is an amazing sign of who we are as baptized Catholic Christians. With how many people do we share a glass or cup? A spouse? Our children? Our very close friends? Here as members of Christ's Body we share from a single cup with people whose names we may not even know. This signifies our intimate relationship through baptism. We are related to others more closely through baptism than we are in any other way. By sharing in the cup together, we act out our true relationship with one another through Christ.

While the consecrated bread is broken, the Lamb of God (Agnus Dei) litany is sung. At one time, when there was much bread to be broken, the song was extended to accompany the action. This part of the liturgy is called "the fraction." From this part was derived the name for the celebration of Eucharist in the early church, "the Breaking of the Bread." Because the wine is poured into individual cups at the Preparation of the Gifts in today's liturgy (instead of during the breaking of the bread), the Lamb of God is usually done as just three lines. In parishes where the community bakes its own bread and there is more breaking to do, it may be extended as long as necessary to accompany the action. The *General Instruction of the Roman Missal* (#43) indicates that we normally kneel in reverence after the Lamb of God, although it allows the diocesan bishop to instruct differently.

Private Preparation

Immediately following the Lamb of God, the priest says some inaudible prayers as part of his preparation for communion. In union with him we do the same. Time is too short for long personal prayer. All that we have done together up to this point has been a preparation to receive Eucharist. We have been actively participating and preparing all along.

Bread: Taken, Blessed, Broken, Shared

At the Last Supper, Jesus took the bread, blessed it, broke it, and shared it with his disciples. At the liturgy, we imitate his actions. At the presentation of the gifts, the bread is taken. During the Eucharistic Prayer it is blessed. It is broken during the fraction rite, and now during communion, it is shared. This is the culmination of our celebration, our communion with Christ and with each other.

Why Bread and Wine?

In the Catholic Church we have emphasized the reality of the bread and wine being truly transformed into the Body and Blood of Christ. Why did Christ choose ordinary elements of a meal as his way of being so intimately present to us? Why is the celebration centered on a meal?

Christ chose to be present to us in these ordinary elements because they are essential to life. Bread, which we refer to as the "staff of life," nourishes us. Wine is a sign of joy. Christ is our nourishment and our joy. The nature of a meal, of communal sharing, is a further sign of what Eucharist is to be for us. In receiving Eucharist, we are joined not only to Christ but also to one another. Through our eating and drinking the elements, which have been transformed into Christ's Body and Blood, we become more closely united to Christ and to his Body, the church. We become transformed into his Body and Blood for others in our daily lives.

Invitation to Communion

The presider shows the consecrated bread and wine to the people and invites us all to come forward to receive. We respond verbally, indicating our humility, reverence, and faith. As soon as the priest (and other ordained ministers, if any are present at the altar) and extraordinary ministers of Holy Communion have received, we begin the communion procession. This should be a true procession, not just lining up as we would in other venues. This is a procession of faith and reverence.

Communion Song

We process forward, singing together to express our unity. The communion song begins when the presider receives communion and continues until all have received. It is an expression of the unity of action of all God's people receiving communion together and expressing their unity with one another and with God.

Receiving Communion

When we approach the minister to receive the Body and the Blood, we first bow in reverence to the divine presence, then respond to the words of the minister, "The body of Christ" or "The blood of Christ" with a sincere

"Amen." When the minister says, "The body of Christ" or "The blood of Christ," there is a deliberate ambiguity. The reference is, of course, to the consecrated bread or wine. It also refers to the person about to receive, who is a member of the Body of Christ. The "Amen" response indicates our affirmation of these truths. It is an act of faith in Christ truly present and an acceptance of our responsibility in being part of his Body.

Parishes and dioceses differ on whether we stand or kneel after we return to the pew. The *General Instruction of the Roman Missal* recommends standing, but it allows the local bishop to decide on the posture for his diocese. Standing makes our communion with one another more apparent. We stand together in solidarity, honoring one another until all have received.

Reserved Eucharist

The early church had no tabernacles. Early Christians did not save consecrated bread for adoration, but they took home extra consecrated bread for those who were not able to attend the communal celebration because of sickness, old age, or some other reason. In this way, the homebound could share in the common banquet through the bread brought from the celebration. Today, we reserve leftover consecrated hosts in the tabernacle to be available for bringing to those who are ill or homebound—and for adoration.

However, the primary purpose of the transformation of bread and wine into the Body and Blood of Christ is not for adoration. The main purpose is so that those who eat and drink at the sacrificial banquet will themselves be transformed, transformed into Christ's Body and Blood for others. Each time we come to the table, we hope to bring that transformation closer to fulfillment. To preserve the integrity of participation in the liturgical sacrifice/banquet, communicants should receive the bread consecrated at that Mass. We are invited to "take and eat," to receive what we have presented and offered, and what has been transformed on our behalf.

Eucharist as Reconciliation

Eucharist is the primary sacrament of reconciliation. We reflect that Christ comes to each of us equally, loves each of us equally, and connects us to himself and to one another in radical intimacy. If we truly believe this, it is impossible not to be reconciled to one another and to God. At the same time, in ritualizing our relationship to one another in receiving from the one bread and the one cup, we also ritualize how we are to be to God's people in the world, a people of reconciliation. We experience in this amazing ritualization of connectedness and intimacy a foretaste of the heavenly banquet. Having this in our consciousness requires that we let go of our anger or bitterness towards others, for whom God exhibits the same welcoming love that God has extended to us.

Silence or Song of Praise

Following communion there may be a brief time of silence to kneel or sit—or to stand and sing a hymn of praise. One or the other may be chosen according to the specific occasion or feast. If there is a time of silence, we can pray in a personal way, perhaps to resolve to grow in some specific way as a result of this celebration. Above all, it is a time to thank God for all we have received during the past week and during this eucharistic celebration. If there is a song of praise, we express our thanksgiving communally. Again, our song should raise the rafters with our praise and gratitude.

Prayer After Communion

Once again, we are invited to pray, this time at the Prayer After Communion. This is another opportunity to form our own prayer interiorly, but we join with one another as we do so. The focus of the prayer, which the presider recites, is to ask that the sacrament we have received together be efficacious in our lives. We respond with a resounding "Amen" to express our affirmation.

Chapter Six
We are Sent Forth

The Concluding Rites form the final segment of the liturgy. They help us transition from the mystery we have celebrated in the liturgy to our life in the world during the rest of the week. We have gathered as Christ's Body, heard God's word, responded in praise and thanksgiving as we presented our gifts, and received them back transformed into Christ's true presence. Now we prepare to go back to our daily lives.

Announcements

Parishes have done much experimentation with the placement of the announcements. Some parishes have put them earlier in the liturgy in the hopes that more people will be present to hear them. However, the usual and liturgically logical placement of the announcements is in the part of the Mass that transitions us back to our workday life during the week. The announcements present us with opportunities for growth or service. These are ways we can put our transformation into practical use within our parish community and beyond.

Greeting and Blessing

One final time we have a dialogue, "The Lord be with you," and its response, "And also with you." We shouldn't lose steam now but give a hearty response to the presider and continue the energy with the "Amen" that follows the blessing. On occasion there is a solemn blessing, which requires a four-fold "Amen" response from us. These solemn blessings reflect the feast of the day and express prayers to God that deserve an exuberant response. Alternatively, there can be what is called the "prayer over the people" followed by the blessing. Either is followed by an energetic "Amen."

Dismissal

Finally the deacon, or in his absence, the priest, uses one of three formulas to dismiss us. All include the words "Go in peace." If the form used is "The Mass is ended, go in peace," our "Thanks be to God" can sound as though we are glad that it is over. Actually, the thanks that we express at this time shows our gratitude for the mystery celebrated and for our being sent out to serve in Christ's name. The energy with which we respond should mirror the energy with which we will accept our roles of service during the week. Energized by our communal celebration and nourished by Christ's own Body and Blood, we are sent forth as Christ sent his disciples to bring Christ to the world and to do our part in preparing for God's reign on earth.

Recessional and Song

The final procession of the liturgy consists of the ministers, which includes, as this book makes clear, members of the assembly. We are part of the recessional as we follow to go out into the world as we have been sent. Most often there is a song, although music is not officially part of the rite. However, an upbeat hymn echoing the focus of the day serves to send us out in higher spirits. During Lent, or at other times during the year, there may be no closing hymn. Sometimes there is silence, or there may be an instrumental accompaniment to our processing out. If there has been a song of praise following communion, it may be desirable to have instrumental recessional music rather than to add another song to the liturgy. If the opportunity to sing is given, we join in the joyful sendoff. If the music is instrumental, we experience it in our hearts. In either case, the focus at this time is on being sent to bring Christ to the world.

Amen! Afterwards, it is a good time to join together for coffee and donuts, or brunch, to experience community in a different way and to regain our energies after the work of celebrating liturgy together. We should feel that we have expended energy in our celebration.

Chapter Seven
The Assembly as an Initiating Community

This book has referred to the community as Christ's Body on earth. One of the aspects of this truth is that we are sent to bring others into our community, to literally incorporate them into Christ's Body with us.

One of the ways we do this is by our presence at baptisms. It has become the norm to celebrate baptisms at Sunday Mass. The idea of a "private" baptism doesn't make sense. The individual is being baptized or incorporated into the Body of Christ, of which we are members. We are the ones responsible for accepting this person and assisting him or her through prayer and example. We can have the opportunity to express this during the baptismal liturgy, not only through our prayers but also in a physical way—for example, by making the sign of the cross on the child when invited to do so. Many presiders now invite not only the parents and godparents but also all those who wish to sign the child with the sign of the cross. By so doing, we express our support for the family and the child. We ritualize our commitment to the newly baptized. We are initiating them into our Christian community. They are joining us on our journey. We welcome them and show our care for them with the sign under which we are united.

The rite of acceptance into the order of catechumens can give us another opportunity to act as members of an initiating community. Ideally, this rite begins outside. Mass begins in the usual way, but after the presider gives his usual greeting, he goes outside to greet the candidates for the catechumenate. It is most meaningful if he invites the whole community to come outside with him to greet them and to bring them into the church building. This action expresses our role in the initiation process and gives those being brought in a feeling of being truly welcomed.

Later in the rite, the priest signs the candidates with the sign of the cross on their foreheads. The sponsors are usually invited to sign the candidates on their senses: ears, eyes, lips, heart, shoulders, hands, and feet. One possible adaptation following this part of the rite is to invite the entire community to come to the candidate nearest them and to sign him or her with the sign of the cross, usually on the forehead. This is a very moving time for the candidates as they experience the positive energy of the community through the meaningful symbol of the sign of the cross.

We can go one step further as members of the initiating Body and become godparents for those being baptized or sponsors for those continuing their initiation through confirmation. We can be sponsors for those in the catechumenate and accompany them on their journey to the Easter sacraments of initiation (baptism, confirmation, and Eucharist) and beyond.

All the sacraments are to be celebrated in the midst of the community. None of the sacraments are intended to be private events. The presence and support of the community are important. All the sacraments give opportunities for the community to respond in prayer and frequently through other actions as well. Even reconciliation, if done within the context of a communal celebration, expresses the community aspect of the sacrament. All pray for one another. All ritualize their reconciliation, if only through the exchange of a sign of peace.

Chapter Eight
What Are These Things?

These are a few liturgical terms you might hear.

Alb: a long white robe with sleeves, worn by the presider, servers, and sometimes other ministers. The alb is white (or occasionally off-white) because it is a garment that represents our baptism.

Altar: the table at which the Liturgy of the Eucharist takes place. We bow to it because it is a symbol of the Body of Christ. It is a primary liturgical symbol and speaks of both meal and sacrifice.

Ambo: the space from which the word is proclaimed, usually a lectern-shaped piece of furniture. The ambo is used for the Scripture readings, the responsorial psalm (which is Scripture), the homily, which relates the Word to our lives, and the intercessions, which are part of our response to the Word we have heard. As the locus of the proclamation of the Word, it is also a primary liturgical symbol.

Ambry: the display area for the holy oils. Usually this is near the baptismal font. It displays the three oils, the Oil of the Catechumens, the Oil of the Sick, and the Sacred Chrism. They are blessed by the (arch)bishop at the Chrism Mass (during Holy Week or the week before) and presented in the parish at the beginning of the Holy Thursday liturgy.

What Are These Things? 47

Baptismal Font: the third of the primary liturgical symbols because it is through the water of the font that we enter into the church community. Ideally, the font is placed near the assembly's main entrance to the worship space in order to maintain that visual emphasis of coming into the community through those waters. However, in some parish churches the normal placement would create poor visibility for baptisms during liturgy. Especially in older church buildings, other physical conditions may exist that prohibit that ideal location for the font. In those situations, the font is located in the front near the sanctuary.

Book of Blessings: a book containing special blessings for various occasions (e.g., thanksgiving for the harvest), objects (e.g., cars, boats, sacred objects), or people (e.g., mothers and fathers on their special days).

Book of Gospels: a large book, frequently elaborately decorated, which contains all the Gospel readings for Sundays and holy days.

Cathedra: the (arch)bishop's chair, located in the cathedral. The name cathedral is derived from this name for the chair. It is a sign of the (arch)bishop's authority in the (arch)diocese.

Chalice: the cup used for the wine to be consecrated.

Chasuble: a large sleeveless vestment worn by the presider at Eucharist. The four basic colors are green, purple, white, and red. Some parishes also have a rose-colored vestment for the third Sunday of Advent and the fourth Sunday of Lent.

Ciborium: a covered container, usually gold or silver, used to store the Body of Christ in the tabernacle.

Cincture: a long cord used like a belt to secure the alb.

Corporal: a square white cloth upon which the bread and wine is placed. It usually has a small cross in the middle or at the bottom. This name comes from the same root as corpus, or body, because the consecrated Body and Blood are placed on this cloth on the altar. Part of its purpose is to catch crumbs.

Credence Table: a small table used for holding things used at eucharistic celebrations.

Cruets: small containers used to hold water or wine.

Incense Boat: the container that holds the incense. It has a spoon for adding the incense to the censor or thurible.

Lectionary: the book containing all the readings for Mass including the Gospels. It usually has a red cover and ribbons. It is not a Bible, but the readings in it are from the Bible.

Paschal Candle: the large candle that is blessed at the Easter Vigil and is used during the Easter season and at baptisms and funerals. In many parishes, it is also burned near the Book of the Names of the Dead during the month of November. It symbolizes Christ, our light, risen from the dead.

Paten: a plate or dish used to hold the eucharistic bread at liturgy.

Presider's Chair: the chair used by the priest during liturgy. It serves as a sign of his leadership role in presiding over the assembly and leading the people in prayer.

Purificator: a rectangular cloth used to wipe and purify the chalices between communicants. It may be embroidered with a small cross.

Sacramentary: a book containing all the prayers for the eucharistic celebration. It has several ribbons and tabs.

Sanctuary: the area containing the altar, ambo, and usually the presider's chair. It is the focus of the action at mass.

Stole: a long narrow vestment worn around the neck and underneath or over the chasuble by the presider. It can also be worn over the alb for non-eucharistic celebrations. A deacon's stole fits over one shoulder and crosses the body, coming together below the waist on the opposite side.

Tabernacle: the sacred space where the consecrated bread is stored.

Thurible: the container in which the incense is burned.

Chapter Nine
Liturgical Seasons

Advent

The beginning of this season starts the church year. This can be confusing because the civil year begins the first of January. The first Sunday of Advent is the last Sunday of November or the first Sunday of December. There are four weeks of Advent, although depending on what day of the week Christmas occurs, the last "week" may be as brief as one day.

The color for Advent is purple. At one time, Advent was viewed as a penitential season. However, the word *advent* means "coming," and it is more properly a season of hope and longing, looking forward to the coming of Christ. Of course, since Christ came in the incarnation over 2000 years ago, the focus of our hope and longing is now tri-fold. We look forward to our "anniversary" celebration of that birth 2000 years ago; we look for the coming of Christ each day in our lives through various persons and events; we anticipate Christ's final coming at the end of time. Advent is a season of preparation, a season of joy. The Alleluia is sung during Advent, although the Gloria is usually omitted until Christmas Eve. An exception is the Feast of the Immaculate Conception, the patronal feast of the United States, which is celebrated with the Gloria.

The third Sunday of Advent is called "Gaudete Sunday," after the first word in the old Latin Introit prayer. (This was the first chant of the liturgy of the day in the Latin Mass. It set the tone for the liturgy to follow.) *Gaudete* is a Latin word that means "rejoice." Many parishes have rose vestments for that day. It is a special day of rejoicing because Advent is roughly half over, and it is almost ...

Christmas

Christmas is more than a day. It is a season that begins with the evening Masses on Christmas Eve and lasts through the feast of the Baptism of the Lord. It includes the Feasts of the Holy Family, the Epiphany, and the Solemnity of Mary, Mother of God on January 1. All these additional feasts, except January 1 are celebrated on Sunday in most years. Depending on the day of the week of Christmas, one or another of the feasts may be moved to Monday. The color for the season is white, a color of joy. The seasons of Advent and Christmas are connected by their focus on the central feast of the Nativity. The day after the Baptism of the Lord begins...

Ordinary Time Following Christmas

This is a relatively brief stretch of ordinary time. Ordinary time gets it's name, not from the lack of specialness of the season, but because the Sundays are designated numerically, for example, the Third Sunday of Ordinary Time. Each Sunday during this season, like each Sunday throughout the year, is celebrated as a "little Easter." The theme of every Mass is the Paschal Mystery, Christ's life, death, resurrection, and sending of the Holy Spirit. Depending on the readings, different aspects of this mystery receive focus and are celebrated. The color for the season is green, the color of hope. Following this brief "low" season is ...

Lent

Lent is a penitential season. The color is purple, a penitential color, except for the fourth Sunday, which is rose, like the third Sunday of

Advent. The priest may wear purple, however, on this day if he so chooses. As in Advent, the rose-colored vestment comes on a Sunday when the old Latin Introit used another "rejoice" word, this time *Laetare*.

Lent is the season to prepare for Easter, to be introspective, and to do a little spiritual "housecleaning." It is a time when we traditionally focus on Christ's sufferings as an inspiration for our own self-betterment. Lent is not, however, a sad time. It is not a season of joyous anticipation like Advent, but it is a season of hope. We know that Christ is risen, and we are looking forward to the celebration at Easter. The focus of Lent is on our need for repentance, reconciliation and forgiveness, and on God's mercy freely granted to us. In many parishes, the penitential rite is emphasized by being sung. The Gloria is not sung, nor is the Alleluia before the Gospel. Another text of praise to Christ is substituted as the Gospel Acclamation.

Lent is also a time of preparation for initiation. The catechumens enter their final period of preparation for their celebration of the sacraments of initiation at Easter. There are a number of rites celebrated during the Lenten season as part of their preparation. There are, for example, the three scrutinies, on the third, fourth, and fifth Sundays of Lent. The scrutinies focus on the catechumens, actually now called the Elect, since they have been elected by the bishop to come to the Easter sacraments. This final preparation period is called the period of purification and enlightenment. During the scrutinies, they are called forward in a spirit of repentance to be prayed for by the assembly. This rite belongs to the entire community. We are members of the community into whose ranks the catechumens will be initiated. It is our job to pray for them and support them. At the same time, we are also in need of repentance and purification. In humility, we appropriate the meaning of the prayers to ourselves as part of our own preparation for the Easter celebration.

The final part of Lent begins with Passion Sunday, formerly known as Palm Sunday. This is the beginning of Holy Week. The color for Passion Sunday is red. It is the color of blood or martyrdom. This color is used for the feasts of martyrs throughout the year. Lent continues until the evening of Holy Thursday, which is the beginning of …

The Triduum

This is a three-day season unto itself. It contains the three most important days of the church year. The entire celebration encompasses the passion, death, and resurrection of Jesus Christ. It is one liturgy taking place over three separate days to focus on the major aspects of this mystery.

Holy Thursday focuses on the night before Christ died and on the Last Supper. The emphasis is on Eucharist but from the perspective of service. This is why the washing of the feet is part of the liturgy as it was part of the Last Supper. Christ's great command is to love one another. The Christian sign of this love is service. Eucharist exists to transform us into Christ's Body for the service of others. The color for Holy Thursday is white.

On **Good Friday**, we hear the reading of the Passion according to John; we have extended intercessions for the church and for all people in the world; we venerate the cross, the wood on which Christ died for us; and we receive communion consecrated at the Holy Thursday liturgy. At no time, even on Good Friday, do we pretend that Christ has not risen. Even in the contemplation of Christ's death, there is no sense of hopelessness as there must have been for the disciples because we know the end of the story. We reflect on the measure of God's love for us as evidenced in Christ's sufferings. We focus on this part of the mystery as we prepare for the contrasting joy of Easter. The color for Good Friday is red.

Holy Saturday brings the Easter Vigil, the mother of all liturgies. It begins with the Service of Light outside. This includes the lighting of the new fire, the blessing and lighting of the Paschal Candle, the procession into the church building following the candle, and the great song of the "Exsultet" sung by the light of the candle. The second part, the Liturgy of the Word, is longer than usual. There are as many as seven readings from the Old Testament chronicling salvation history (each with its own responsorial psalm), an epistle reading, and finally the Gospel proclamation. The third part is the Liturgy of Baptism, which includes the Litany of the Saints, the blessing of the water in the font, the renewal of baptismal promises, and baptisms and confirmations. The fourth part, Liturgy of the Eucharist, is the part most like a regular Sunday Mass—except for the first communions of the newly initiated. This liturgy is usually two-and-a-half to three hours long, and can be longer. It is as glorious as one might expect from an event that celebrates the victory of life over death and the promise of eternal salvation. The color is the white of joy and continues through the …

Easter Season

The Easter Season begins with the Easter Vigil and continues until the end of Pentecost. There were forty days of Lent leading up to Easter and fifty days of Easter to continue the joyous celebration. As were Advent and the Christmas season, Lent and the Easter season are connected, the season of preparation with the season of rejoicing. It is a high season of the year, full of Alleluias and an environment full of white and gold and flowers. The color for Pentecost is the red of the fire of the Holy Spirit. The Monday after Pentecost begins …

Ordinary Time Following Easter

Once again we are back into Ordinary (ordinal or "green") Time until we begin the liturgical year with Advent once more. The plunge into Ordinary Time comes gradually as we begin with two major feasts, Trinity Sunday, and the feast of the Body and Blood of Christ, formerly known as Corpus Christi. Throughout the year, various feast days may take the place of a Sunday in the numbered progression, but mostly it is a low season, leading us back to the greater intensity of the Advent season.

Conclusion

The ministry of the assembly is of vital importance. Other ministers derive their roles from the members of the assembly. What we do when we participate in liturgy as members of the assembly affects the rest of the Body assembled there. What we do is not just for ourselves but for all.

It just might be that after years of full participation as members of the assembly, we may want to take on an additional role. That would be the time to consider becoming a lector, a music minister, an usher or greeter, or an extraordinary minister of communion. Or a "background" ministry, such as working on the environment, might be appealing. Whatever course we take, we will always be, first and foremost, a member of the assembly, and that will always be our most important ministry.

Selected Bibliography

Deiss, C.S.Sp., Lucien. *The Mass*. Collegeville, MN: The Liturgical Press, 1992.

Fabing, S.J., Robert. *The Eucharist of Jesus: A Spirituality for Eucharistic Celebration*. Phoenix, AZ: North American Liturgy Resources, 1986.

Keifer, Ralph A. *To Give Thanks and Praise: General Instruction of the Roman Missal*. Washington, D.C.: The Pastoral Press, 1980.

Keifer, Ralph A. *To Hear and Proclaim: Introduction to the Lectionary for Mass*. Washington, D.C.: The Pastoral Press, 1992.

International Commission on English in the Liturgy. *Book of Blessings*. Collegeville, MN: The Liturgical Press, 1989.

International Committee on English in the Liturgy, Inc. *General Instruction of the Roman Missal (Third Typical Edition)*. Washington, D.C.: United States Catholic Conference, Inc., 2003.

International Commission on English in the Liturgy. *The Sacramentary*. New York: Catholic Book Publishing Co., 1985.

International Commission on English in the Liturgy and Bishop's Committee on the Liturgy. *Rite of Christian Initiation of Adults*. Chicago: Liturgy Training Publications, 1988.

National Conference of Catholic Bishops. *Lectionary for Mass*. New Jersey: Catholic Book Publishing Co., 1998.

Smolarski, S.J., Dennis C. *Sacred Mysteries: Sacramental Principles and Liturgical Practice*. Mahwah, NJ: Paulist Press, 1995.

United States Conference of Catholic Bishops: Bishops' Committee on the Liturgy. *Introduction to the Order of Mass: a Pastoral Resource of the Bishops' Committee on the Liturgy*. Washington, D.C.: USCCB Publishing, 2003.

United States Conference of Catholic Bishops: Bishops' Committee on the Liturgy. *Sing to the Lord: Music in Divine Worship*. Washington, D.C.: USCCB Publishing, 2007.

"Who Me, A Minister?"

Even if you're not a priest, a deacon, a eucharistic minister, a lector, or a minister of hospitality, you're still a minister. If you attend any liturgy, even if all you think you do is sit in a pew, you're a minister. Maybe the most important one of all.

In fact, even if you serve in other liturgical ministries, your primary ministry is the "ministry of the assembly."

The Ministry of the Assembly explains your role in the liturgy step by step. It develops the concept that you and other members of the assembly are called to minister to each other. It's a practical guide to the what, when, how and why of your part in the liturgy. Whether you're a neophyte or a lifelong Catholic, this book is designed to help you achieve a deeper understanding of the liturgy and to continue to grow in more conscious, active, and full participation.

Caroline Thomas has been involved in liturgy planning since the early 1970s, leading to an MA degree from the University of Santa Clara in 1992. She has worked in parishes as the director of liturgy for more than 14 years, and continues to be passionate about the potential of the liturgy to transform its participants.

 Resource Publications, Inc.
160 E. Virginia St. #290
San Jose, CA 95112

ISBN 978-0-89390-675-7

Ministry/Liturgy / $4.95